SUGAR SKULL COLORING BOOK

50 Fun Sugar Skull Illustrations

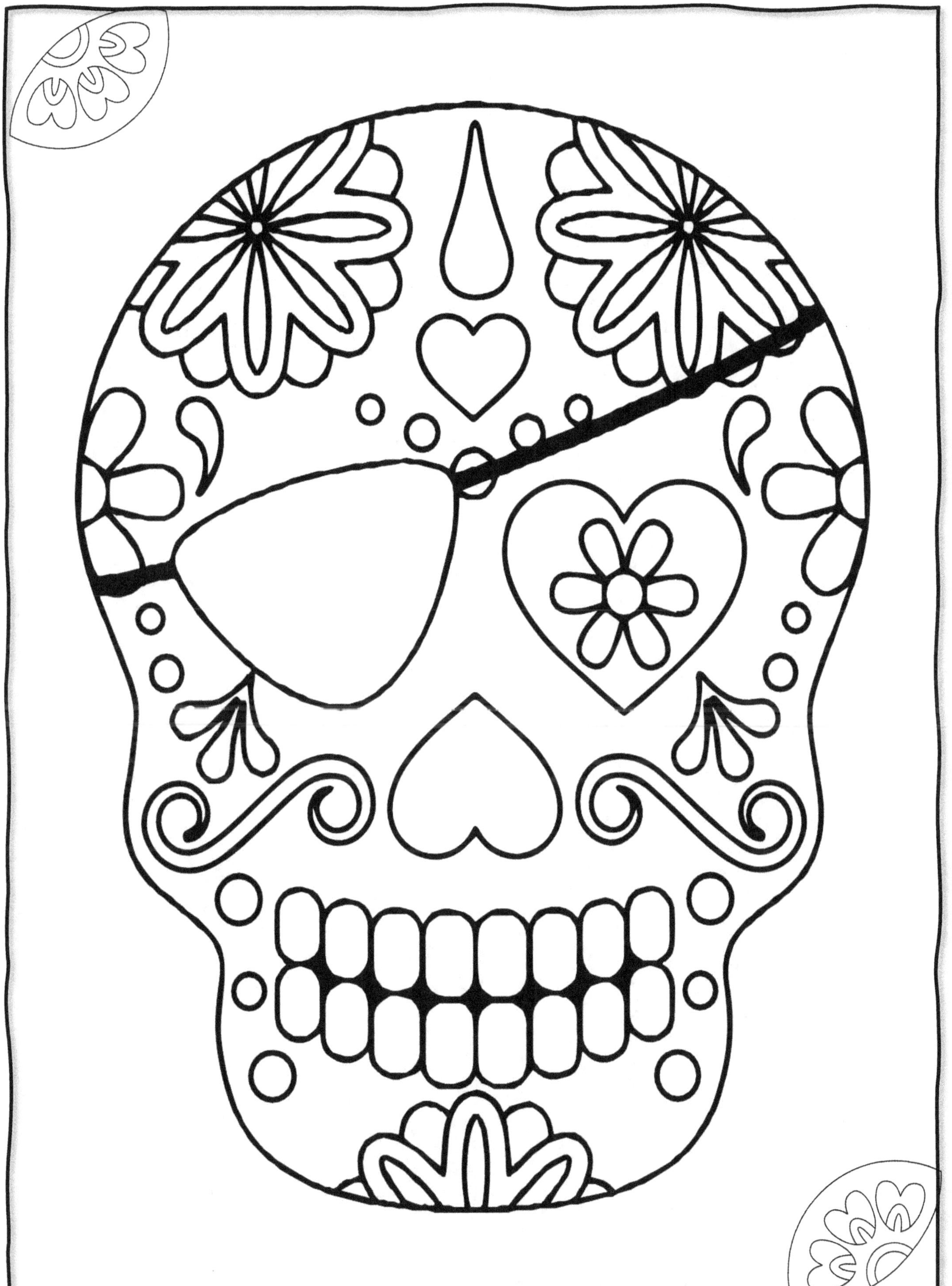

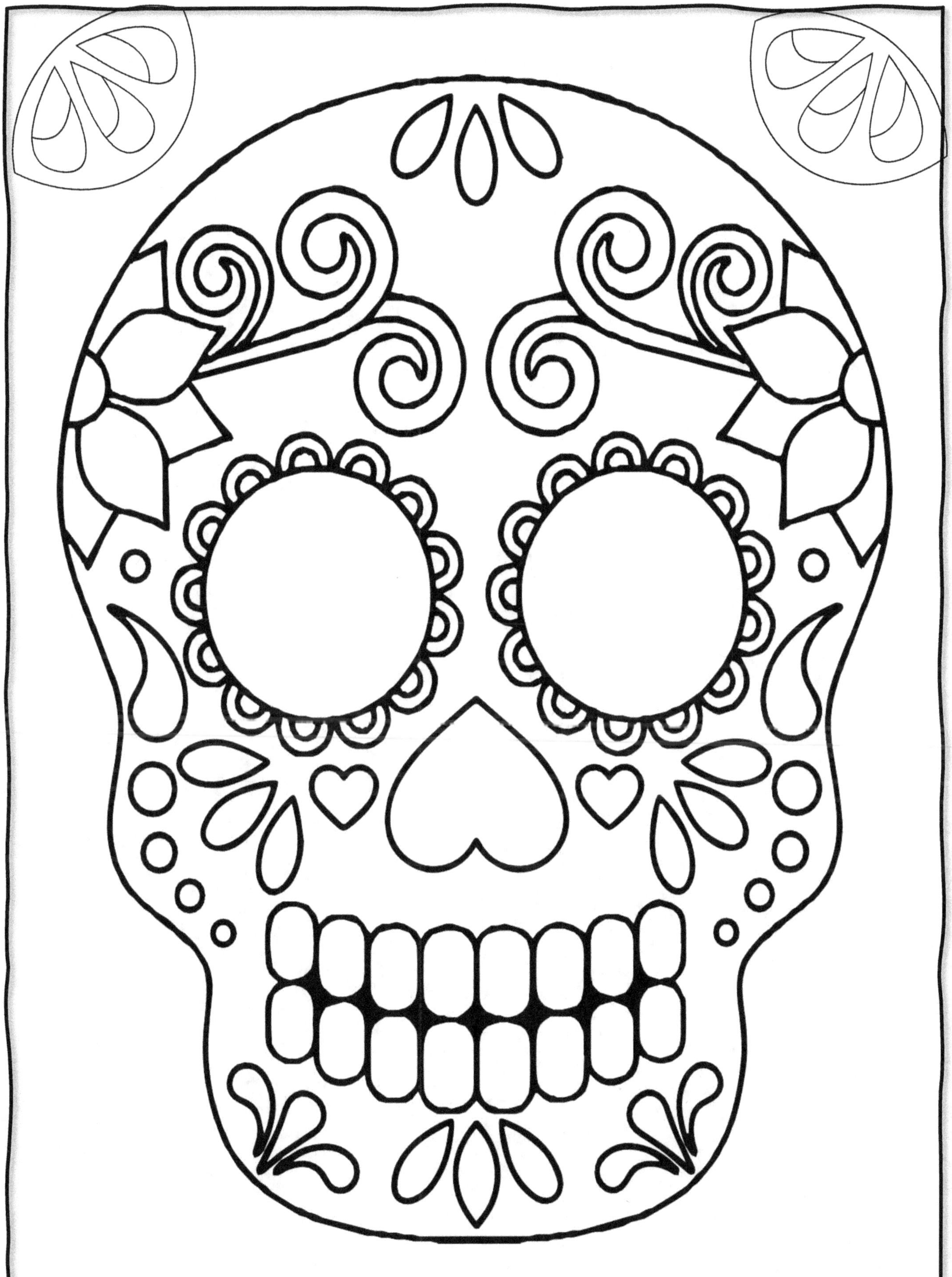

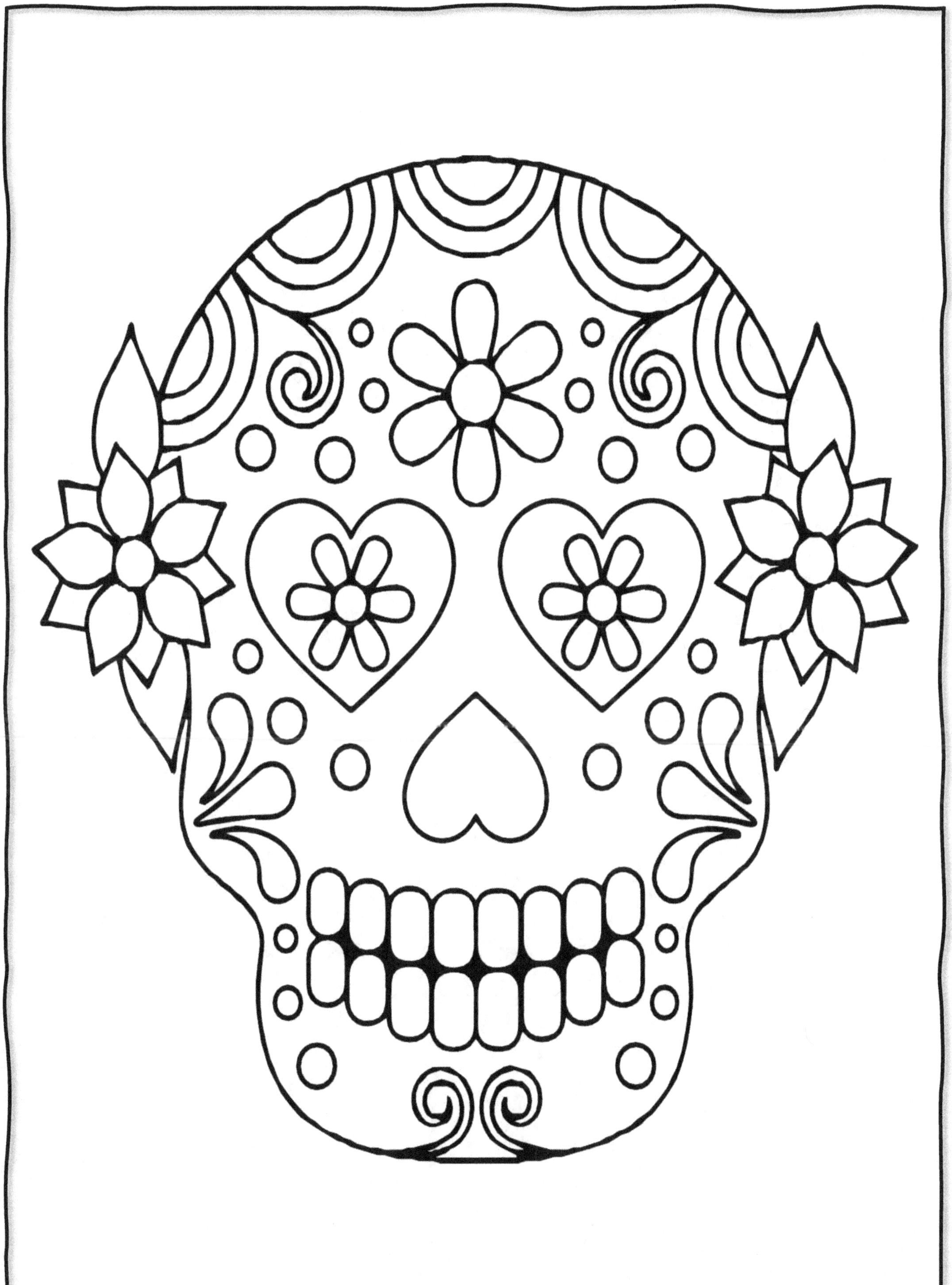

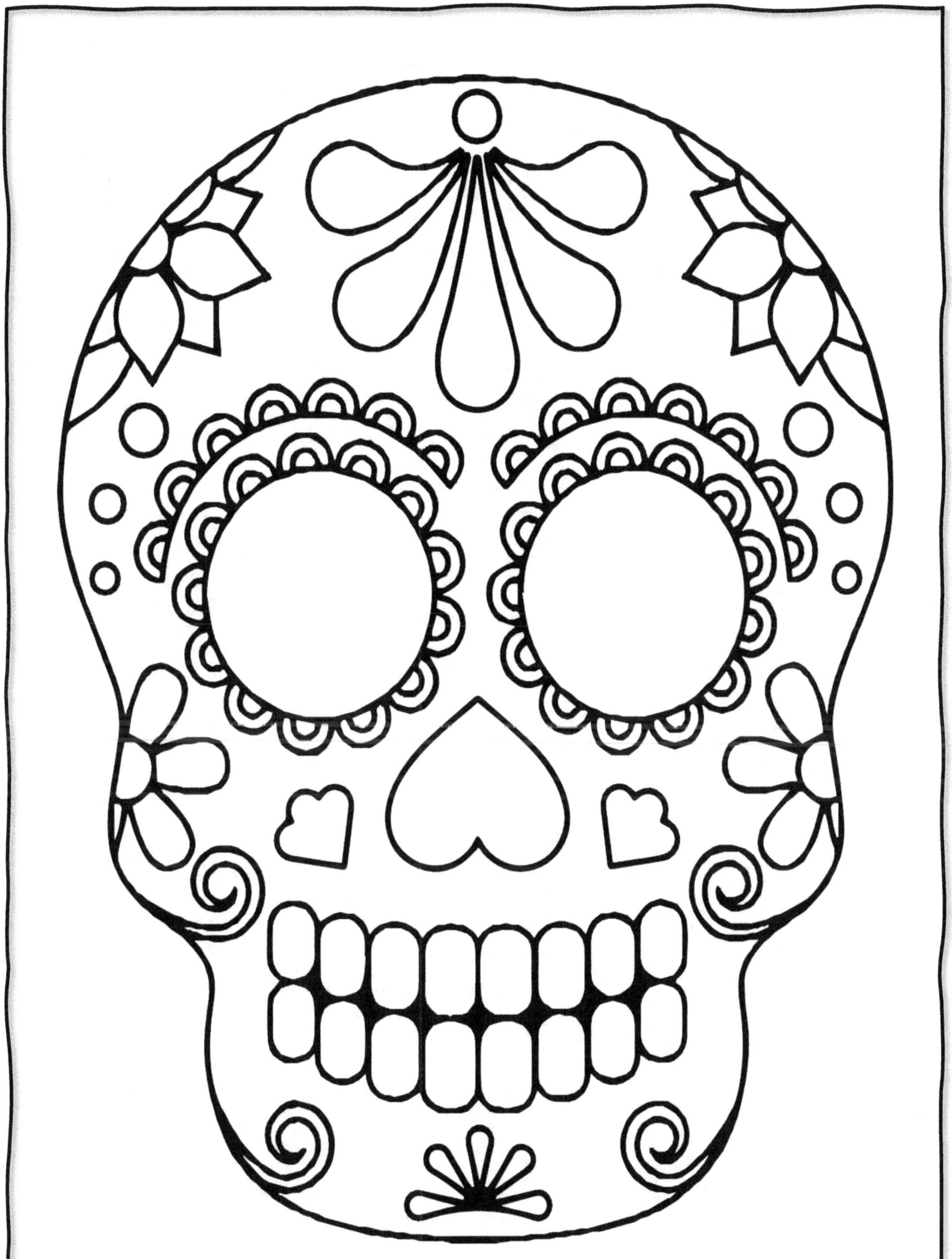

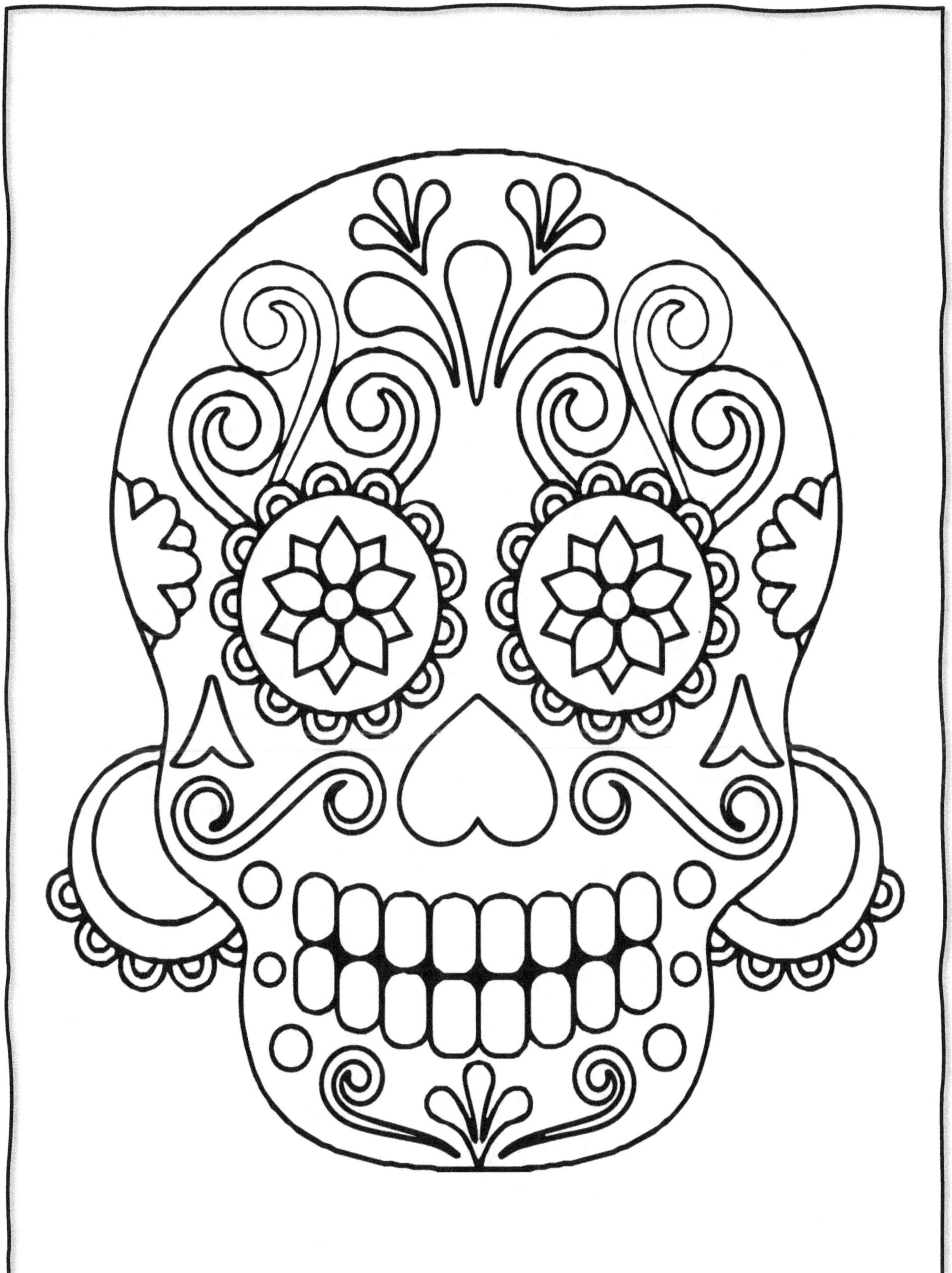

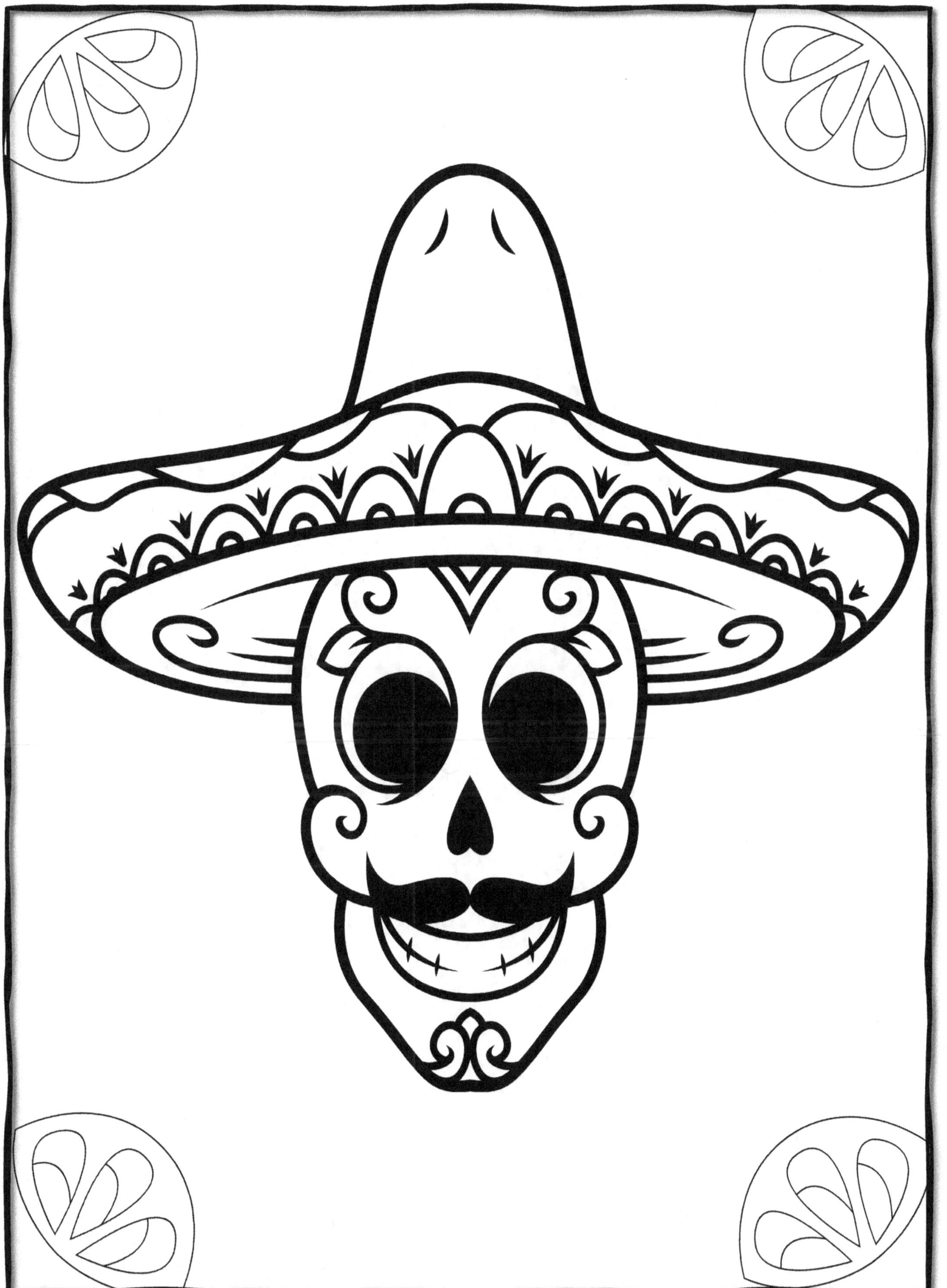

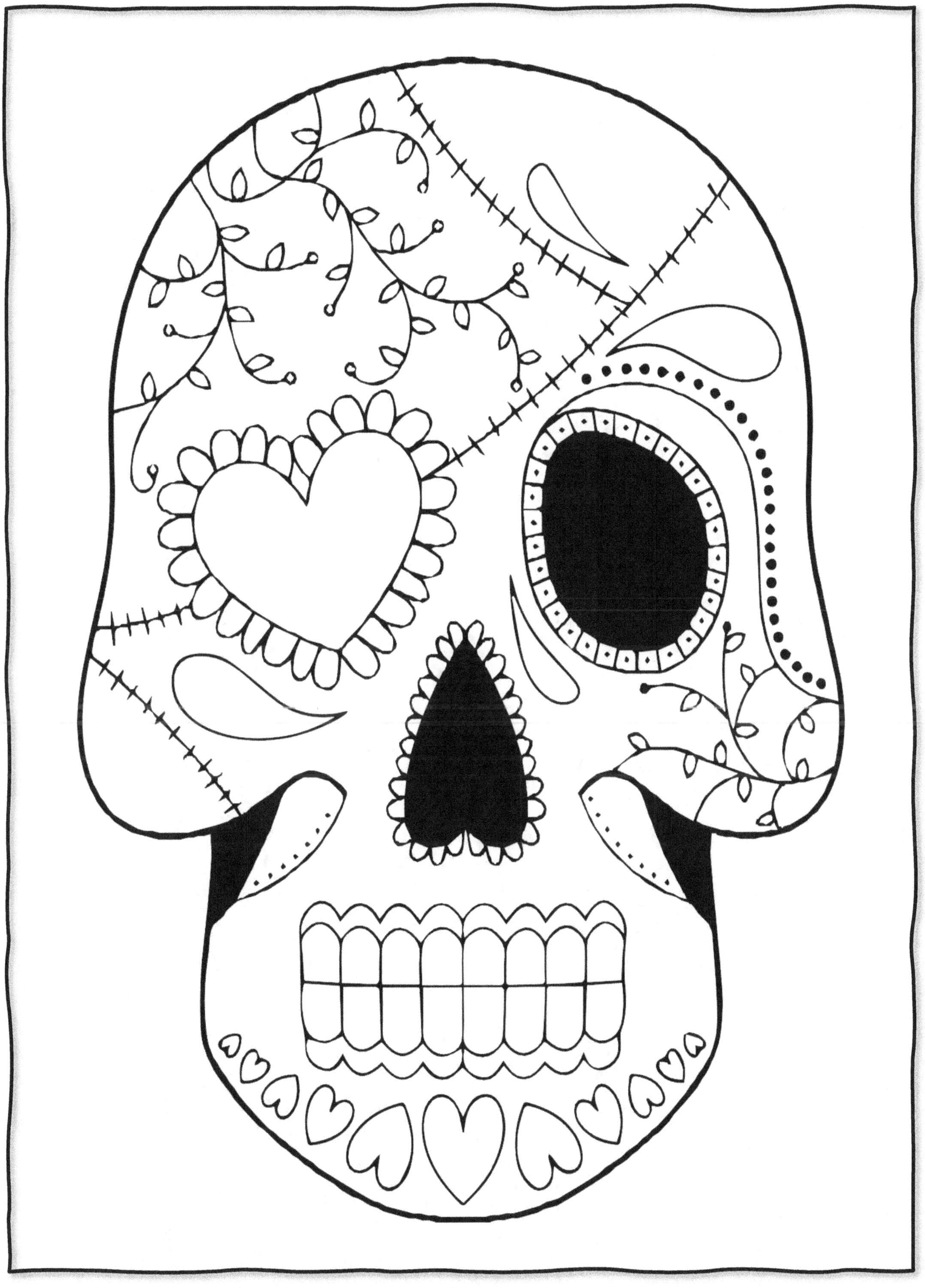

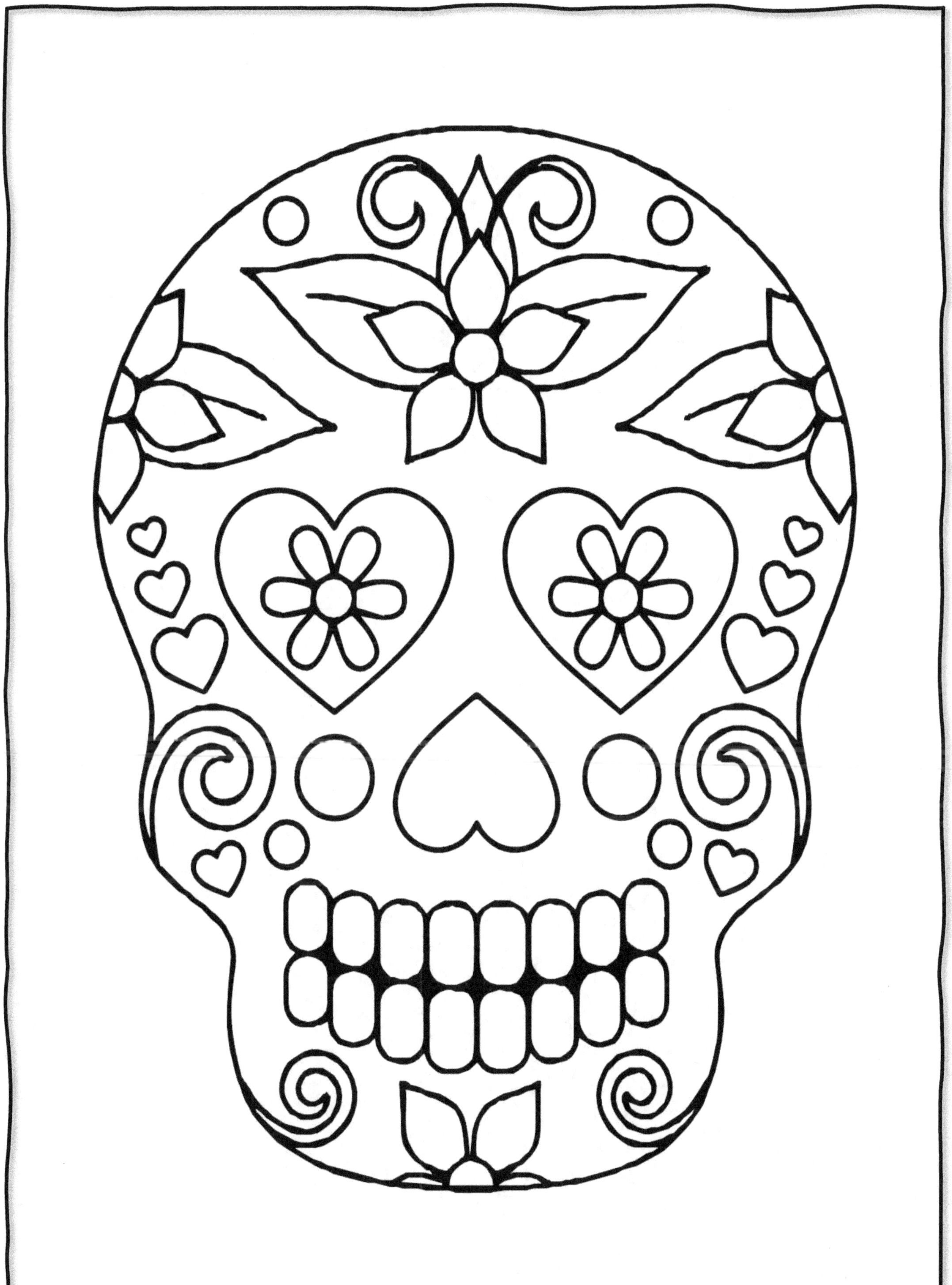

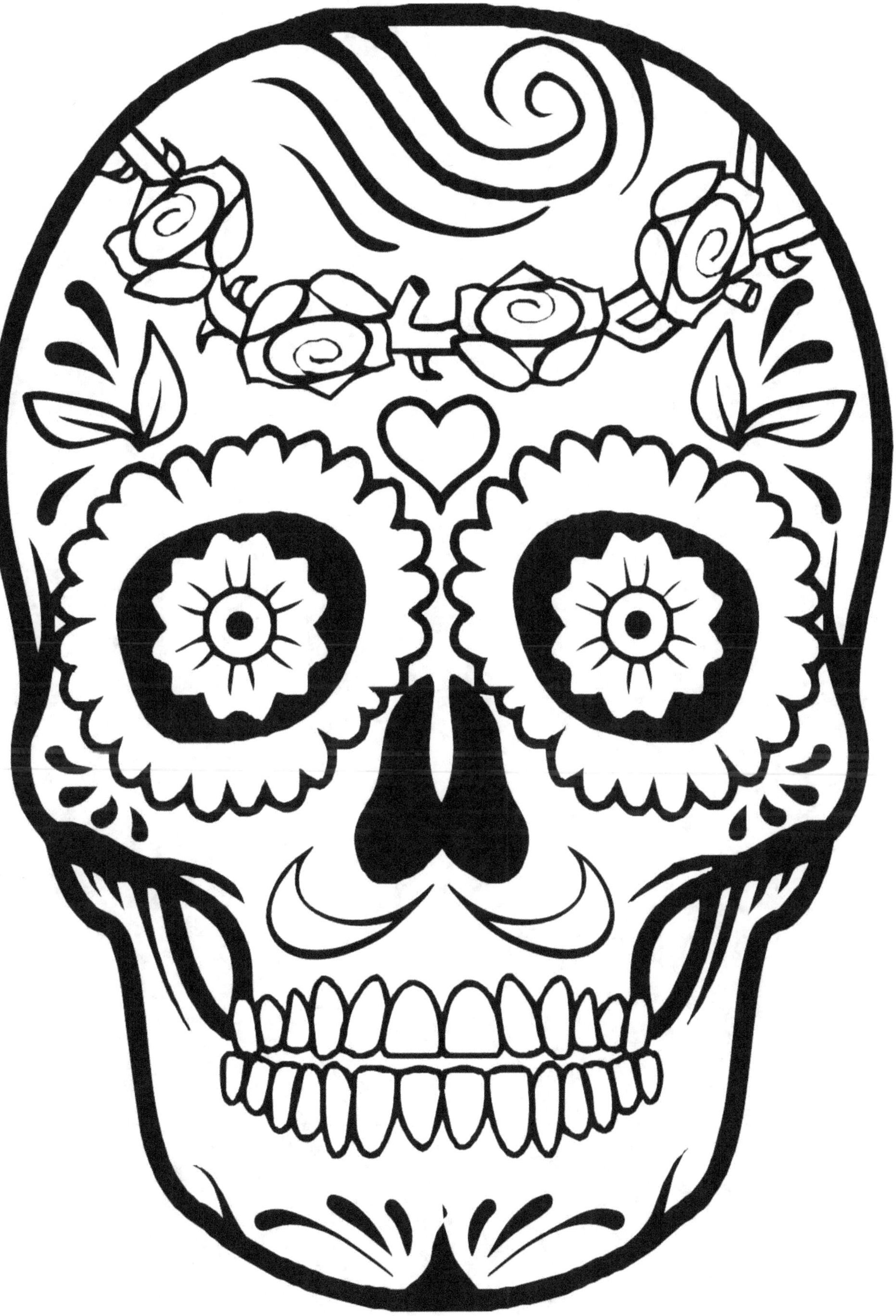

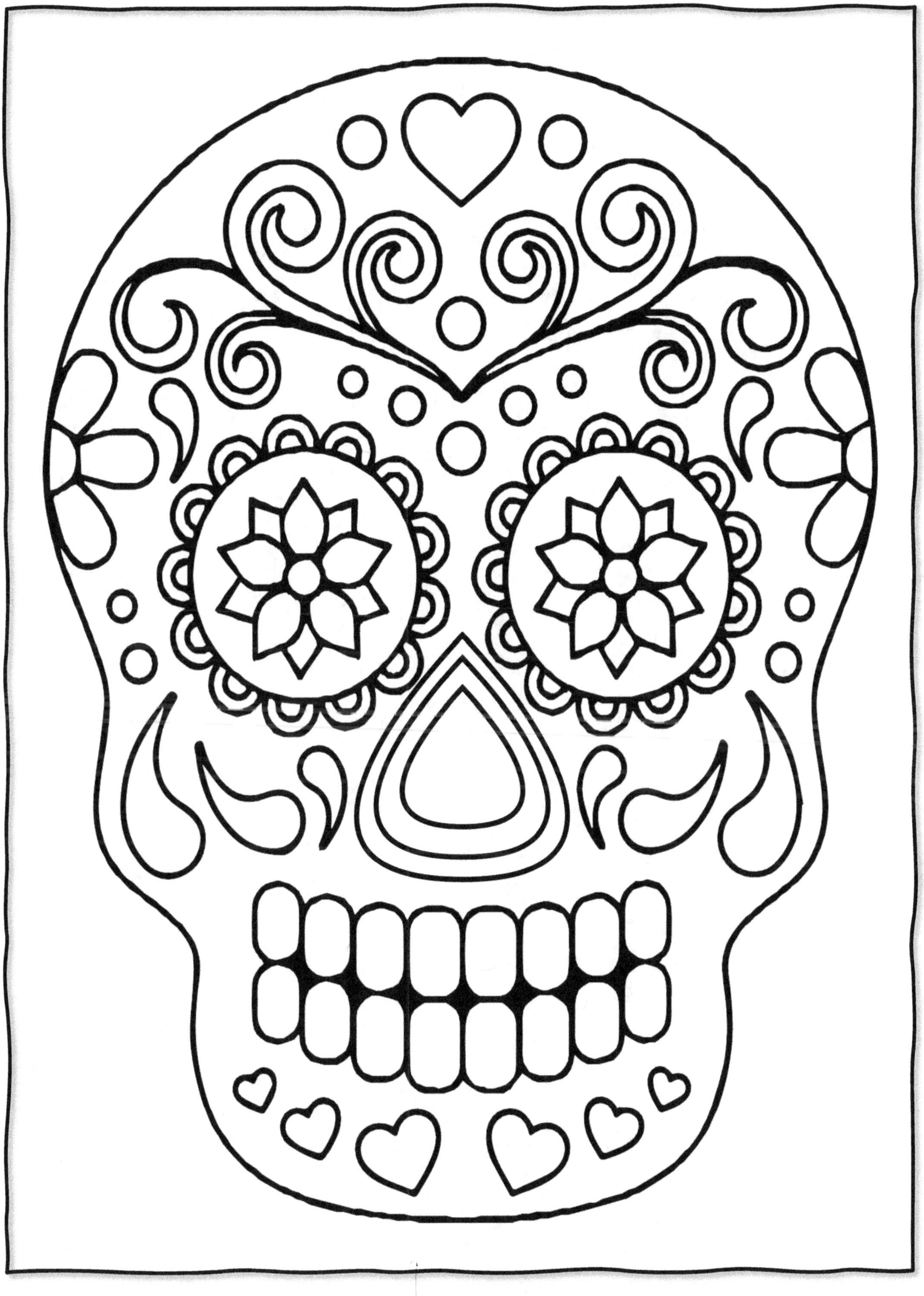

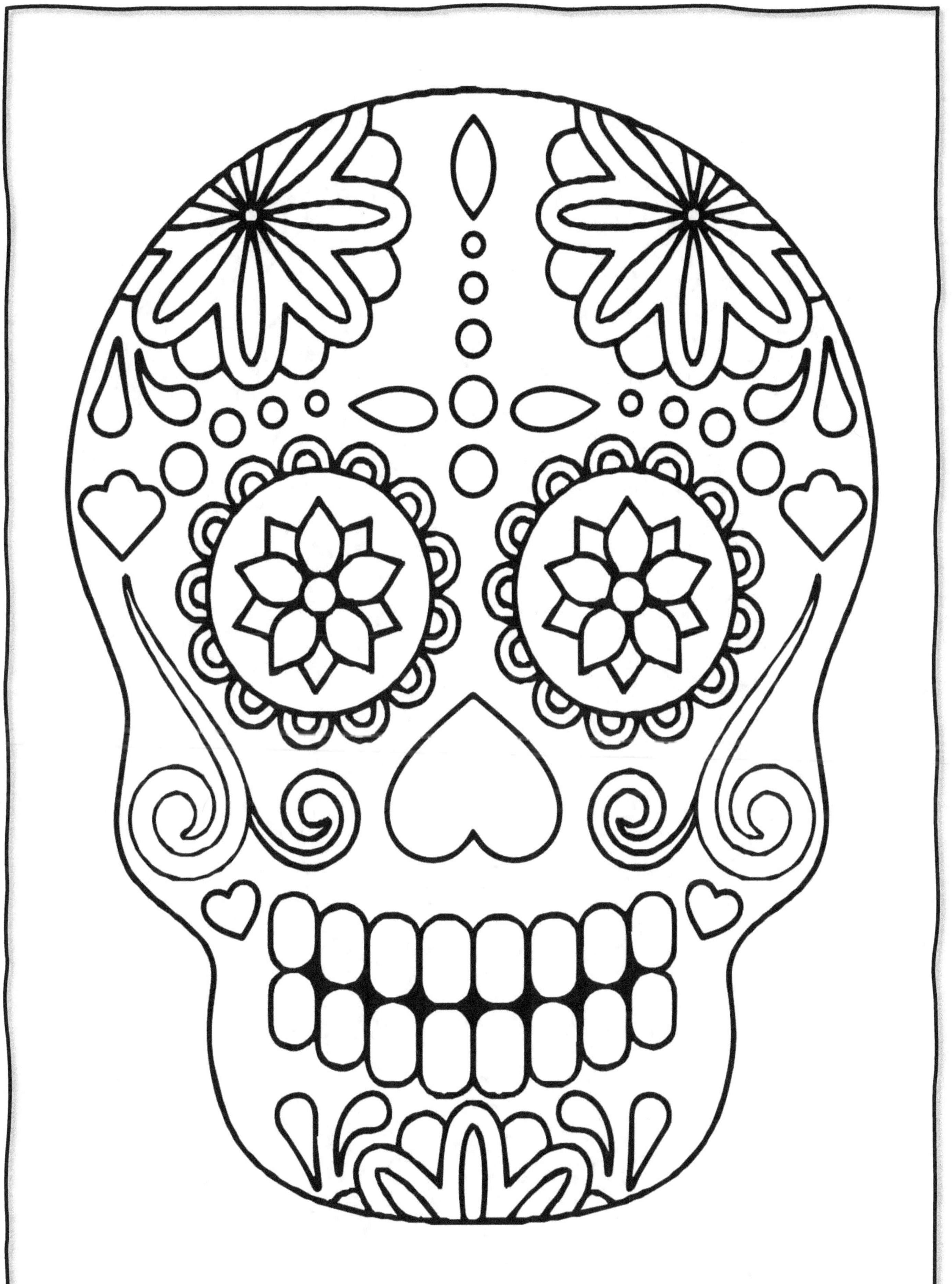

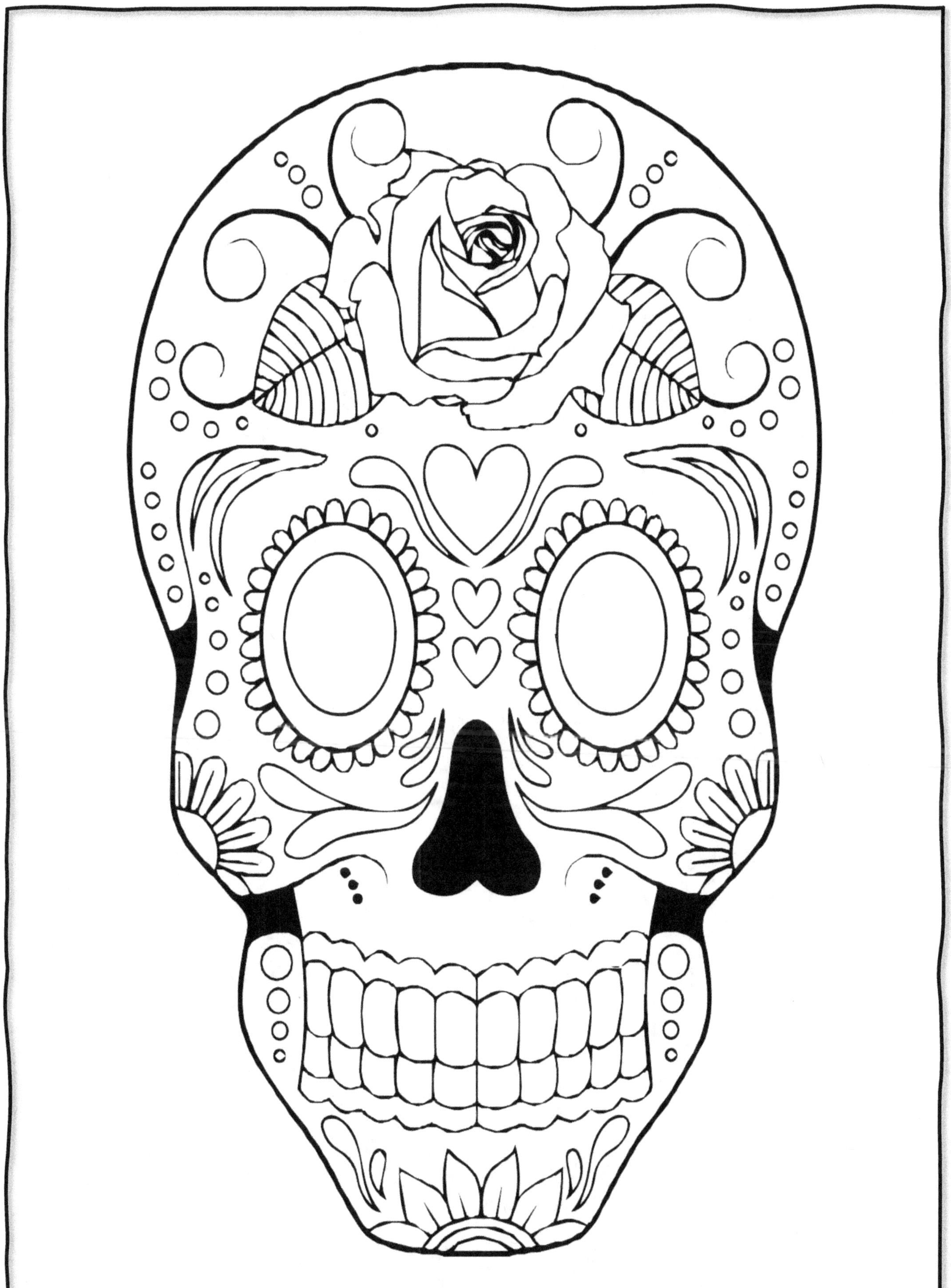

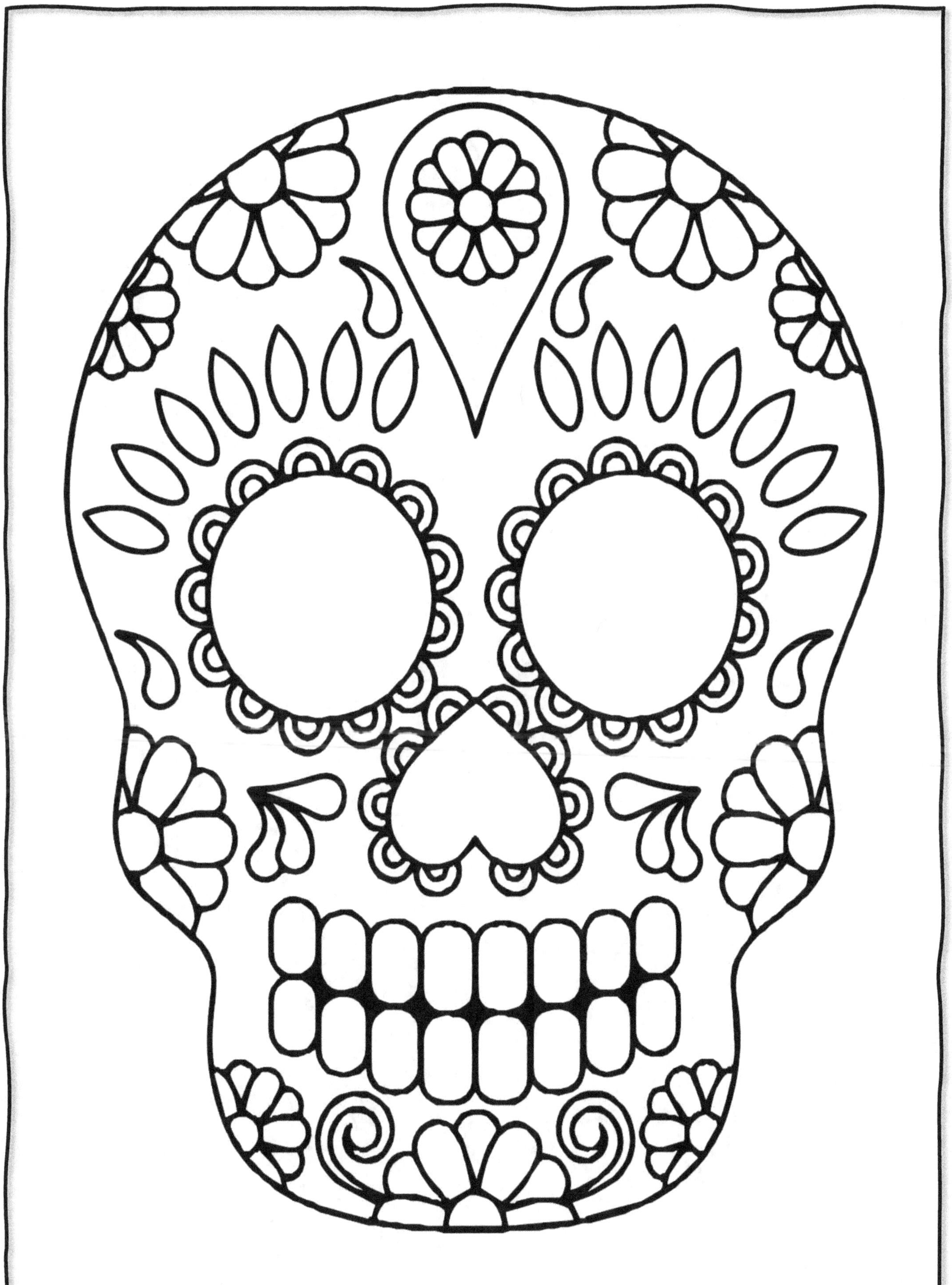

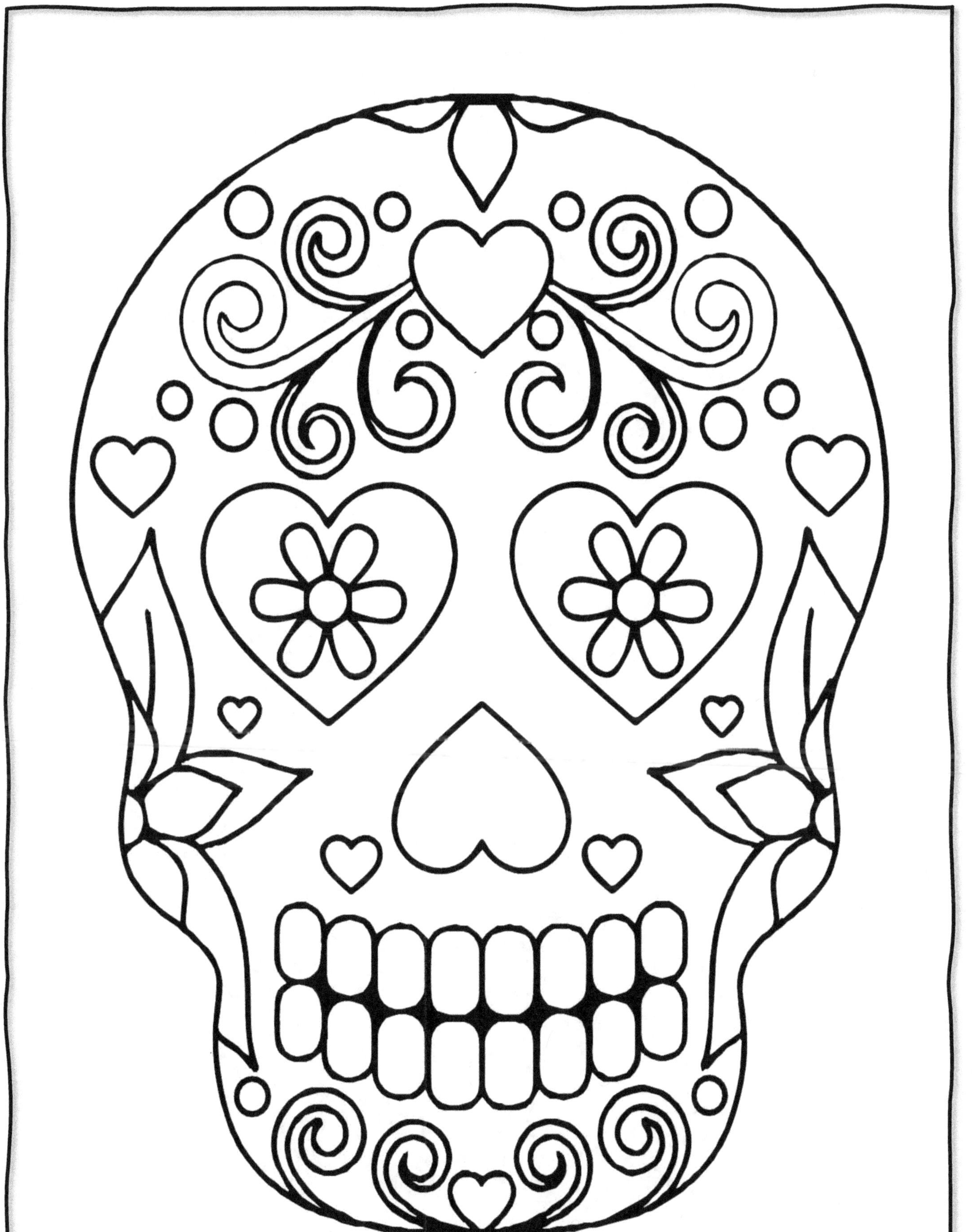

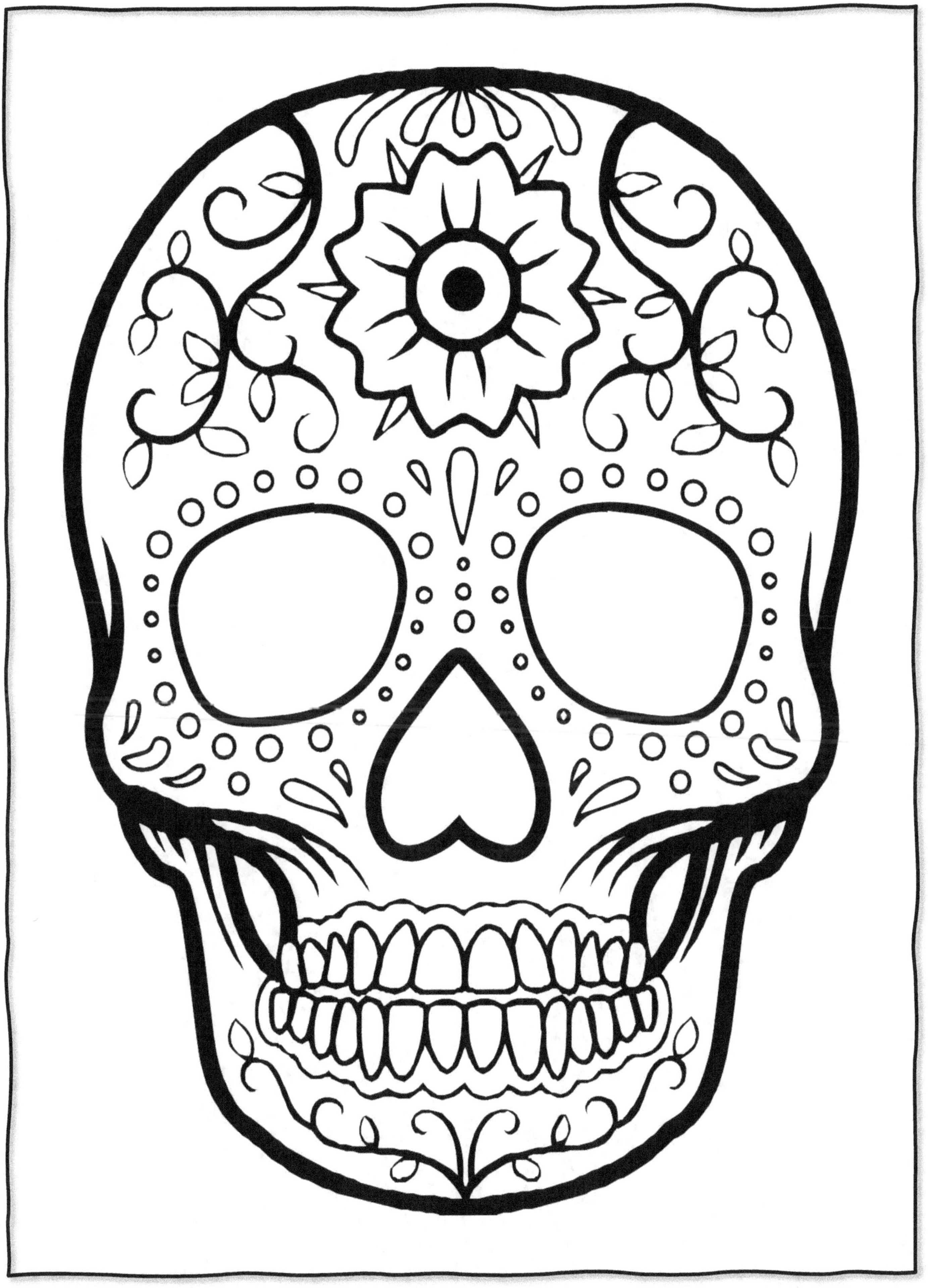

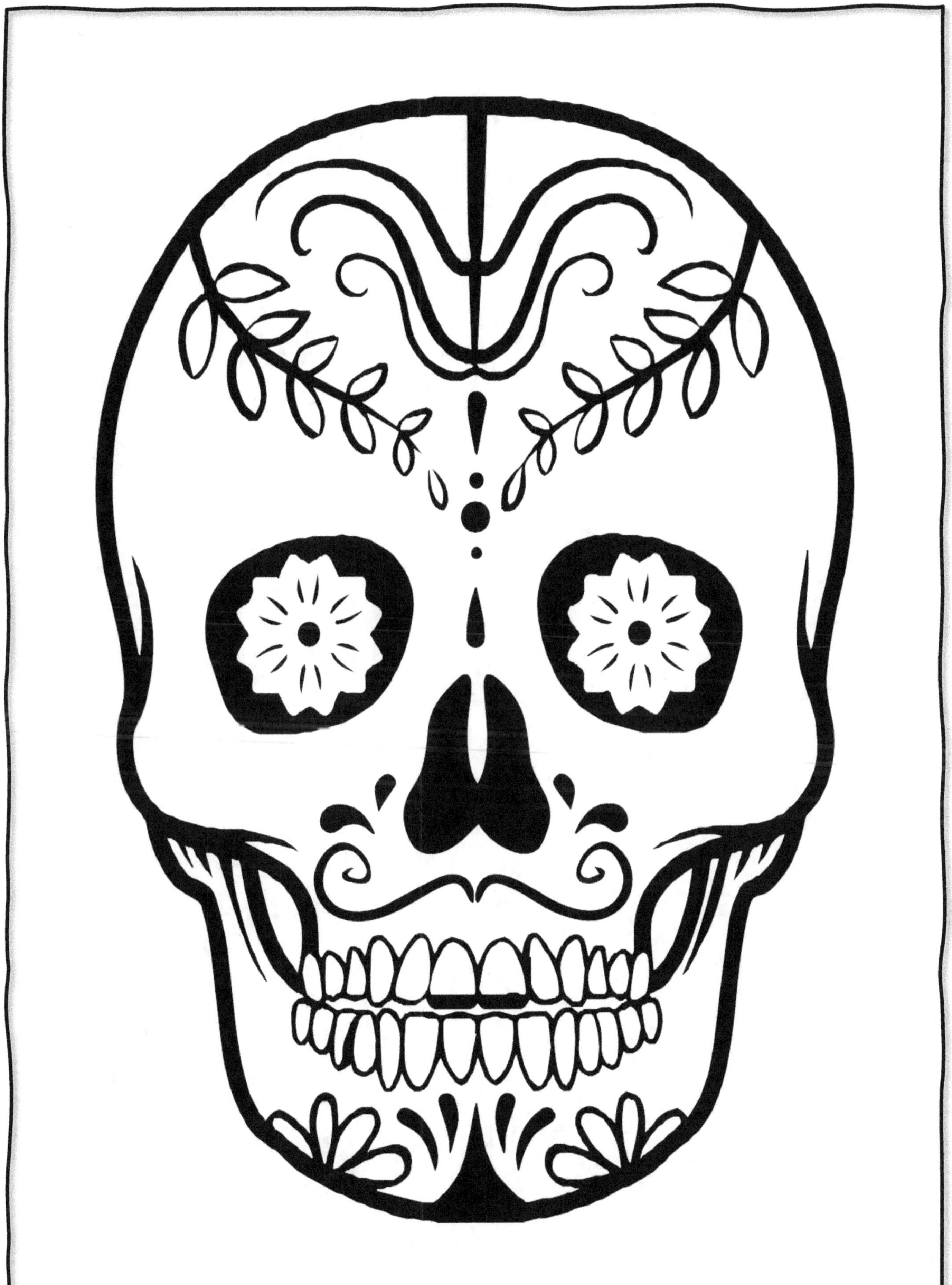

www.ingramcontent.com/pod-product-compliance
Lightning Source LLC
Chambersburg PA
CBHW082124220526
45472CB00009B/2293
* 9 7 9 8 6 8 2 6 8 4 0 2 1 *